Dramatic Monologues Listening Comprehension

Resource material for listening and fluency practice

Colin Mortimer

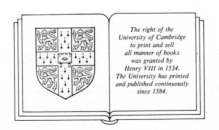

Cambridge University Press
Cambridge
London   New York   New Rochelle
Melbourne   Sydney

Published by the Press Syndicate of the University of Cambridge
The Pitt Building, Trumpington Street, Cambridge CB2 1RP
32 East 57th Street, New York, NY10022, USA
296 Beaconsfield Parade, Middle Park, Melbourne 3206, Australia

© Cambridge University Press 1980

First published in 1980
Fifth printing 1986

Printed in Great Britain by
Richard Clay (The Chaucer Press) Ltd,
Bungay, Suffolk

ISBN 0 521 22923 5 Resource Book
ISBN 0 521 22934 0 Cassette

Monologue 23: Answers

1. A patient.
2. A hospital ward.
3. Another patient (John).
4. Spots.
5. Unique.
6. The distribution of his spots.
7. A student doctor.
8. The specialist (dermatologist).
9. a) A nurse.
   b) Apply something to the spots.
10. He decides to defer the request as that particular nurse goes off duty shortly and will be replaced by a very good-looking nurse. He would prefer to be treated by her.
11. Visiting time commences.
12. The speaker's wife.
13. Visiting time is not intended as an opportunity for visitors to talk about ailments: the focus of attention is the patient.
14. John's wife.
15. That the new patient's spots were distributed like his – in which case he would no longer be unique.

Monologue 24: Answers

1. Probably a board room. Perhaps an office.
2. Probably the chairman, or managing director.
3. Mr Peterson, who appears to head a team of consultants or advisers.
4. Other members of the board, or other members of the management team.
5. Mr Peterson's offer.
6. Lucid, challenging and interesting.
7. Many of those present are sympathetic to it.
8. Men, materials and expertise.
9. The ability to meet their tight deadlines.
10. The estimates.
11. Human relationships.
12. Something along the lines of:
    we are unable to accept your offer
    we are not in a position to take up your offer
    we shall have to decline your offer
13. To decline the offer as tactfully and painlessly as possible.

Contents

Introduction

This book, aimed at upper-intermediate and more advanced
students, provides 24 monologues for listening comprehension,
together with questions and answers. The book is suitable for use
either in class or for self-instruction. It is accompanied by a cassette
on which the monologues are recorded.

Each monologue is dramatic in the sense that it presents a
character who addresses a listener or listeners in a particular situation.
(One passage, in fact, is a soliloquy: the speaker is talking to himself.)
Though they are scripted, the monologues simulate many of the
characteristics of natural spoken language.

The monologues aim to help students to learn to listen
intelligently, picking up clues to situation, context and personality
in the way a native speaker would. The students' main tasks are
to say who the speaker and the listener are, to identify the situation,
and to understand what happens in that situation. It is hoped that
in undertaking these tasks, students will increase their responsiveness
to implicatory language, and develop in particular an ability to
recognise the references of pronouns.

The monologues can be used in various ways. In general,
however, it is best to listen to the whole monologue once or twice
before listening to parts of it. *Students should not look at the text of
the monologue until they have attempted to answer the questions.* Answers
are provided at the back of the book. Where a question has no
definite answer, likely or possible answers are suggested. After
answers have been checked, the monologue should be listened to
again.

Teachers may wish to provide additional questions on the
monologues. Though many of such questions will be on detail, one
general question which can usefully be asked is 'What do you think
happened next?'

The monologues can, of course, be used as a basis for oral or
written summary.

An alternative way of presenting a monologue from time to
time – for variety – is to play only a phrase or two of the tape, then
stop it and ask:

What did he/she say?
then elicit as much information as possible from the class about the speaker, the listener and the situation before starting the tape again and revealing a few more phrases.

Monologue 1

You know, a lot of people find this sort of situation quite frightening. Terrifying, in fact. Anyway, the light's still on. Oh – spoke too soon. What *is* happening, I wonder? And the trouble is, I'm not sure there's anyone left in the building now. I'll try the telephone again, if you like, but I should think it's not working. And, as I say, I'm not sure even if it *is* there'll be anybody there. Now this bottom button's the alarm, I seem to remember. No. Doesn't ring. Can't, I suppose, if there's no power. There *is* that little seat in the corner, you know, if you'd like to sit on it. No, sorry, *that* corner. Ouch! No, it's nothing – just my foot. My fault entirely. Well, you can tell I know this thing pretty well. Should do. I've worked here for twenty years. Never replaced it – though they service it, of course. Afraid I haven't got any sandwiches or anything. I *do* have some on the way *up*, of course. Well, the canteen isn't very exciting, is it? And it's *very* expensive, don't you think? We're supposed to be going to the theatre, actually. Ballet. Used not to like ballet, but somehow I seem to be getting used to the idea in my old age. Prefer it to opera, in many ways. Alice has *always* been keen, of course. Oh – one thing to remember is that there's no problem about *air*: well, you can feel the draught yourself, can't you? One advantage of being old-fashioned, I suppose. I say – aren't you whatsisname's new secretary? He's a lucky chap. You should see mine. Anyway, shall we both just give one more shout?

Monologue 1 : Questions

Listen to the monologue and then answer the questions.

1. In what place is the speaker talking?
2. Who is the listener?
3. What has happened?
4. How well do the speaker and listener know each other?
5. 'Oh – spoke too soon.'
   What event prompted this remark?
6. 'No, it's nothing.'
   What event prompted this remark?
7. 'Well, you can tell I know this thing pretty well.'
   What is 'this thing'?
8. 'I *do* have some on the way *up*.'
   Explain this remark.
9. What two comments does he make about the canteen?
10. 'We're supposed to be going to the theatre.'
    Who does 'we' *not* include?
11. 'Alice has *always* been keen.'
    a) Who is Alice?
    b) What is she keen on?
12. 'One advantage of being old-fashioned, I suppose.'
    a) What is old-fashioned?
    b) Why is this an advantage?
13. 'You should see mine.'
    What or whom does 'mine' refer to?
14. 'Shall we both just give one more shout?'
    What does this remark imply has already happened?

Monologue 2

Well, as I say, I can fully understand that when your colleague is
away on holiday, someone has to take his place, and of course I'm
very glad that you were able to spare the time to see me. After all,
looking after your *own* practice must be difficult enough, especially
with all this sickness about. And you still have about six out there,
after me, so I mustn't keep you. But when you say you don't think
I should *take* them any more and you're not going to *prescribe* any
more – well, what am I supposed to do? Though I suppose you
could be right. You may very well be right, in fact. Certainly, last
night – well, actually I was watching television. And the funny
thing was, it was my favourite programme, too. Anyway, the next
thing I knew, I had pins and needles in my arms and legs, and I felt
stiff and cold. The programme had finished, of course – long ago –
it was half past three, would you believe it? So, as I say, you may be
quite right – perhaps I *don't* need them. But, well, I've sort of got
used to them, you see – though only one each night, you understand.
And, anyway, what will *he* say when he gets back?

Monologue 2: Questions

Listen to the monologue and then answer the questions.

1. In what place is the speaker talking?
2. Who is she talking to?
3. Which three single words help you particularly to know who she is talking to?
4. What does the speaker want from the listener?
5. How has the listener reacted?
6. 'Only ... each night, you understand.'
   Fill in the blank.
7. 'And the funny thing was . . .'
   What was funny. Why?
8. What did she have in her arms and legs?
9. Who does the pronoun 'he' refer to?
10. What is 'out there'?
11. Who are 'out there'?
12. In a few sentences, describe the speaker's reaction to the listener's decision.

Monologue 3

So that's it, Charles, I'm afraid. I can't tell you how sorry I am –
how sorry we *all* are. Needless to say, if there'd been any
alternative solution . . . But I think you'd be the first to agree things
had reached the stage when it just had to be one or the other. So,
having looked at it from all points of view, that's what I've
decided, harsh as it may seem. However, I don't need to tell you how
greatly we've valued your contribution – may I say your *unique*
contribution – here. And I hope you'll find satisfaction in the
knowledge that the organisation is what it is, er . . . very much
because of what you have helped to make it. And I mean that. As
for compensation – I've set out our proposal here, and I think you'll
find everything satisfactory, even generous. Well, as I say, there it is.
You know, Tim's quite a nice fellow, really. Frankly, I could never
quite understand why you two . . . Anyway.

Monologue 3: Questions

Listen to the monologue and then answer the questions.

1. What are the speaker and the listener both members of?
2. What is the relationship of the speaker to the listener?
3. What is the listener's name?
4. What has the speaker decided?
5. Who does 'one or the other' refer to?
6. What has led to the speaker's decision?
7. Which phrase suggests that the situation leading to the decision has developed over a period of time?
8. What does the speaker offer the listener in addition to praise for his 'contribution'?
9. What word is used to describe his 'contribution'?
10. 'I've set out our proposal here.'
    What does 'here' refer to?
11. 'Well, as I say, there it is.'
    What does 'it' refer to?
12. What phrase at the beginning of the monologue means roughly the same as 'there it is', as used in this situation?
13. 'Frankly, I could never understand why you two ...'
    Suggest a completion for this sentence.
14. What is the speaker's overall aim in this monologue?

6

Monologue 4

Frankly, I've been delighted. As you know, I decided to give it up ten years ago. I put them all in the attic – all fifty or sixty of them – to gather dust, and forgot about them. Then I just happened to meet *him* one day in a bar, entirely by chance, and we got talking about this and that, and, well – to cut a long story short – he went to have a look at them, and this is the result. It's for two weeks. And it's devoted entirely to my work. Doing very well, too, as you can see from the little tickets on about half of them. You know, now that they're hanging on the wall like this, with all the clever lighting, and glossy catalogue, and the smart people, they really don't seem anything to do with me. It's a bit like seeing old friends in new circumstances where *they* fit and you *don't*. Now, you see *her*? She's already bought three. Heard her saying one day she's 'dying to meet the man'. Afraid she'd be very disappointed if she did. Interesting, though, some of the things you overhear. Some know something about it. Others know nothing and admit it. Others know nothing and don't. By the way, I heard someone say the other day that the 'Portrait of a Woman' reminded her of you, you know. So you see, you're not only very famous, but – as I keep on telling you – you haven't changed a bit.

Monologue 4: Questions

Listen to the monologue and then answer the questions.

1. In what place is the speaker talking?
2. What did the speaker decide to give up ten years previously?
3. Who is 'he'?
4. 'he went to have a look at them'
    a) What were 'them'?
    b) Where were they?
5. 'It's for two weeks.'
    What is 'it'?
6. What do the 'little tickets' signify?
7. 'she's "dying to meet the man" '
    a) Who is 'she'?
    b) Who is 'the man'?
8. 'Others know nothing and don't.'
    What does 'don't' mean?
9. In a few sentences say what we know about the listener.
10. Why does the speaker feel 'they really don't seem anything to do with me'?

Monologue 5

I *know* there's nothing I can do about it. Of *course* he can't put it back again! But at least surely I have the right to let off steam a bit, don't I? I mean I *told* him, didn't I? I *told* him! Just a bit here, I said. Just a little bit here, and just the tiniest bit there. And nothing at all off here. Nothing. Well, then I closed my eyes, as I always do. That's part of the satisfaction, I always think – it's, well, it's relaxing. But he kept on snipping and snipping and suddenly I came out of my daydream and looked in the mirror. Ugh! Well, I told him what I thought of him, *I* can tell you. I mean if it'd been my first time it would've been different. But I've been going for months, and it's always been perfect. Anyway, never again! And don't try to tell me it's not too bad, because it's terrible – you know it is. Look at it! Just look at it! You can smile if you like, but I'll tell you one thing: we're not going this evening – or at least *I'm* not going. I can just see their faces if I did. I can just see your *sister's* face, especially. Anyway, they'd prefer to have you on your own. And you know what I think of your mother's cooking. Tell them I've got a cold. Well, I soon *will* have, won't I?

Monologue 5: Questions

Listen to the monologue and then answer the questions.

1. Who is the speaker talking to?
2. 'I *told* him!'
   Who did she tell?
3. What has he done?
4. What was the speaker doing while this was happening?
5. Why does she find it hard to believe that this has happened?
6. 'Anyway, never again!'
   What does she mean by this?
7. How does the listener react when she tells him to 'look at it!'?
8. Where does the speaker *not* intend to go that evening?
9. Whose reactions does she particularly wish to avoid?
10. What two additional reasons does the speaker give for not going?
11. 'Well, I soon *will* have, won't I?'
    She soon will have what?

Monologue 6

But everybody has his own way of going *about* it, and my way isn't your way, Alan, I know. But who's to say it isn't just as good in the end? Even so, I'll admit *mine* puts more of a strain on you. I mean, *last* time, I had to go to bed for two days afterwards, I was so exhausted. And *you* don't get this continual nagging sense of guilt in the previous weeks that I get – because whereas you're doing a bit every day in your orderly manner, I'm doing *other* things – but my mind isn't *completely* on them, you know. There's always a part that's a bit anxious. And then one day the anxiety suddenly turns to panic, and I have to go through the panic stage – which is horrifying. And then I start. Six a.m. to midnight to begin with. A bit of time off for meals of course, but less and less. And then the day before the *first* one, hardly any sleep at all. And like that until they're all finished. No pills, of course – don't believe in that sort of thing. Well, perhaps an occasional aspirin. But there's still four weeks, isn't there? So, I'm off for the weekend. You would too, if you knew someone like Katie. Well, no, perhaps you wouldn't. By the way, I wouldn't mind having a look at your notes when you've finished that. Haven't read it yet. Anyway, must be off now. Look, it's good of you to worry about me, but don't. I always *have* got through, so far, haven't I? Bet you a meal at Jack's I get a distinction and you don't!

Monologue 6: Questions

Listen to the monologue and then answer the questions.

1. What are the speaker and the listener?
2. What is the listener's name?
3. In one word, what is the main topic of the monologue?
4. 'everybody has his own way of going *about* it'
   What is the listener's way?
5. What stages does the speaker always have to go through before he settles down?
6. How much sleep does he have before 'the first one'?
7. Does the speaker ever take pills?
8. How many weeks remain before the event with which the monologue is concerned?
9. Who is Katie?
10. What might the listener do, according to the speaker, if he knew someone like her?
11. What is 'Jack's'?
12. 'I always *have* got through, so far.'
    Supply a synonym for 'got through'.
13. 'I wouldn't mind having a look at your notes when you've finished that.'
    What is 'that'?
14. 'Even so, I'll admit *mine* puts more of a strain on you.'
    a) What does 'mine' refer to?
    b) Who does 'you' refer to?

Well, why shouldn't I be quiet? And why shouldn't I be shy? And if you say I *am* pretty, why shouldn't I be? People always seem to think anybody in my position has to be bossy and aggressive – but there are plenty of *men* who aren't. And nobody thinks *they* can't cope. Mind you, it's taken a long time to convince them I know what I'm doing and that I mean what I say. But it's coming along very nicely now and even the accountant seems to accept me. The *deputy* manager has done from the start – he's been marvellous – and not in the way you think. What I mean is he's just accepted it as a normal thing and judged me on my merits. However, to come to the point: it wouldn't work, would it? I *know* you're the best man in the business in your line, and I know you're just what we need. And I know the deputy manager has said O.K. Perhaps if I'd known you were you and you'd known I was me, things would've been different last night – though *I've* no complaints. But on this, I *do* mean what I say – and it *is* my decision.

Monologue 7: Questions

Listen to the monologue and then answer the questions.

1. Who is the speaker?
2. With what three adjectives has she been described by the listener?
3. What have these characteristics *not* led him to expect?
4. 'there are plenty of *men* who aren't'
   Plenty of men who aren't what?
5. Who was the *first* to accept the speaker?
6. Who seems to have been the *last*?
7. What does the speaker want to be judged on?
8. What is the listener hoping for?
9. Give three reasons why he could reasonably expect to get it.
10. What, according to the speaker, might have made a difference to the course of events the previous night?
11. 'it *is* my decision'
    What is the decision?
12. 'it wouldn't work'
    What does she mean by this remark?
13. What is her attitude to the events of the previous night?

Monologue 8

Well, now, ladies and gentlemen, that was our last item, and all that remains for me to do is to thank our performers sincerely on behalf of us all for the pleasure they have given us this evening. And of course I must express thanks to those who've worked behind the scenes. And especially our producer. But most of all I want to say thank you to all of *you* for coming here this evening and supporting this event, especially in such weather. I think perhaps I should take this opportunity to renew my sincere apologies to those sitting in the back rows. We've made temporary repairs to the roof, but unfortunately the rain tonight was unexpectedly heavy, and we're grateful to you for your understanding and cheerful good humour. I may say that we *had* hoped that temporary repairs would suffice. But we were recently informed by our surveyor that the whole roof will have to be replaced: which is of course a severe blow when you think it's only five years since we replaced the roof of the church *itself*. And so we shall be having *another* concert soon, I hope. But assuming we do, and it's as successful as tonight's splendid show, you'll appreciate that the need for more routine effort will still remain. And this is why I hope that when you receive my letter after the service tomorrow, you will respond to the best of your ability. Well, now, the hour is late, and it only remains for me to say . . . Er . . . I notice that those of us at the front now seem to be getting . . . So I'll wish you all a speedy goodnight. Er, can we have some more . . . Well, yes. Yes, *teapots* will be better than nothing Mrs Maxwell, if everything *else* is at the back! Quick as you can, please. The floor, you know.

Monologue 8: Questions

Listen to the monologue and then answer the questions.

1. Who is the speaker?
2. In what place is he speaking?
3. Who is he speaking to?
4. What has been the occasion?
5. Who does he wish to thank most of all?
6. What has happened to those in the back rows?
7. How have they reacted, according to the speaker?
8. What has already been replaced?
9. What will have to be replaced?
10. According to whom?
11. What will 'the letter' be?
12. When will they receive it?
13. 'those of us in front now seem to be getting . . .'
    Suggest a one-word completion for this sentence.
14. 'Er, can we have some more . . .'
    Suggest a one-word completion for this sentence.
15. 'The floor, you know.'
    Explain what the speaker means by this remark.

Monologue 9

Everybody agrees I'm just ordinary. My face is ordinary, my voice is ordinary, my clothes are ordinary. Everything about me is ordinary. 'What's Frank like?' they say. 'Frank? Oh – you know. Ordinary,' they say. Now look at that man two rows in front. He's not ordinary. In fact I can't see anybody apart from me who is. Even this fellow next to me. Quite ordinary on the whole, I suppose. But there's something a bit . . . something a bit odd about his mouth. Mustn't catch his eye. Might start a conversation. Don't want that. Interesting that he was just in front of me in the queue. They looked in his bag, they looked in his pockets – made him take his shoes off even. Mm – they've nearly finished with the food – though she didn't take my glass when she collected my tray. Ah – she's pressed her button again. Probably wants another gin and tonic. Had four already. Or is it five? Not bad, though. At least, not in *this* light. Good – some of them are getting their blankets down now. I reckon that in about half an hour it'll all be quiet. And then . . . Of course they looked in *my* briefcase too. Didn't look *here*, though, did they? Oh, no. Hah! Though they think otherwise, I know very well who those two in the *back* row are. Noticed them when I went to the toilet. But they won't shoot. Not as long as I have *this* in my hand, they won't. And it's so small. Marvellous what they can do these days. Just about now, if I were sitting in funny mouth's seat and not by the aisle – just about now, I could probably look down and see the mountains gleaming in the moonlight. I like that. Mm. Well, now I must go over my speech again. Mustn't forget what my *demands* are, must I?

Monologue 9: Questions

Listen to the monologue and then answer the questions.

1. What is the speaker's name?
2. Who is he talking to? *Think carefully.*
3. What word does he say best describes him?
4. Where does this scene take place?
5. What does he intend to do?
6. 'Don't want that.'
   What doesn't the speaker want?
7. 'They looked in his bag.'
   Who are 'they'?
8. 'she didn't take my glass'
   Who is 'she'?
9. 'she's pressed her button again'
   Who is she?
10. 'Not bad, though.'
    Explain this remark.
11. 'Didn't look *here*, though.'
    Explain this remark.
12. Who is 'funny mouth'?
13. 'Marvellous what they can do these days.'
    What causes him to make this remark?
14. Who are the two sitting in the back row?
15. What is the 'speech' to which the speaker refers?

I admitted I couldn't do many words a minute. But he said that didn't matter too much. And I said I didn't have much experience of handling files, and I'm not much good on the telephone. But he said never mind my dear, nothing to worry about, you can always learn. I thought the others were *much* more what he'd have in mind – you know, neat, alert and obedient – towers of strength in a crisis. Then this nice lunch I told you about. Travel – that was going to be the thing. Lots of travel. He thought I'd be good at that. And I do like travel, he's perfectly right. So come along back, he says, and we'll get you to sign on the dotted line and you can start tomorrow, if you want. Which I was just about to do, when the phone rang. He picked it up and said, 'Oh, I didn't *see* you there, dear. You must've been at a corner table.' Then he listened for a *long* time, said that even so he'd be home late, and put it down. Drummed his fingers on the desk for a bit. Then he said, giving me that smile, there's been a change of plans, and he'd have to pursue 'an alternative line'. Did he mean by that he was going to take someone else, I asked him, and he said yes he was. On the other hand, how about dinner? The travel was still a distinct possibility, he thought. Hm! Well, how did *you* get on, in your neat blouse? – which I will borrow tomorrow for the next one, if you don't mind. Did they take you? Oh, well, never mind. Let's make some egg and chips.

Monologue 10: Questions

Listen to the monologue and then answer the questions.

1. What have the speaker and the listener been aiming to do during the day?
2. Have they been successful?
3. At what skills does the speaker claim *not* to excel?
4. What seems to be in her favour?
5. What were the characteristics of 'the others'?
6. Who is 'he'?
7. What did he say he thought she would be good at?
8. Where did they go before she went 'to sign on the dotted line'?
9. Who did he speak to on the telephone?
10. 'I didn't *see* you there, dear.'
    Where was 'there'?
11. What remained of the offer, after the telephone call?
12. What does the speaker want to borrow?
13. Did she go out to dinner? How do you know?
14. What does the listener probably *do*, between the speaker's saying 'Did they take you?' and 'Oh, well, never mind'?

Monologue 11

I think I should start off by making it quite clear that I don't intend
to lecture in the normal way. If what you're expecting me to
produce is a neat exposition plus handouts and whatnot which you
can give me straight back in the examination, then you'll be
disappointed – you needn't bother to come. Well, I suppose you *do*
need to, as I'm required to check the attendance. No, I see these
sessions more as an occasion for trying, if I can, to act – how shall
I put it? – to act as a *catalyst*: to try to bring about the kind of
exciting, life-long relationship between yourselves and the subject
that I myself have been privileged to experience. And I may say
I'm surprised – pleasantly surprised – to see that your numbers are
so large. This particular subject is not one which in the past has
attracted much interest at *undergraduate* levels. Quantitatively
speaking, I mean. In fact, during the last five years, a total of six
is all we've managed. Well, to focus our attention, I propose to
write the name of our subject on the blackboard, thus. And then
we shall consider its derivation. Now. Oh – is there something
wrong? By the way, you *did* get the notice about the change of
rooms, didn't you?

Monologue 11 : Questions

Listen to the monologue and then answer the questions.

1. In what place is the speaker talking?
2. Who is the speaker?
3. Who are the listeners?
4. What is the speaker's general aim in this monologue?
5. What is he 'required' to do?
6. Why is he surprised?
7. '... not one which in the past has attracted much interest at *undergraduate* levels'
   What meaning does the speaker probably intend to convey by the extra stress on 'undergraduate'.
8. In one word, what does the speaker hope to act as?
9. What does he *not* intend to provide?
10. What derivation is he about to consider?
11. In a sentence or two explain the significance of 'the notice'.

Monologue 12

He comes in every other Tuesday and he brings back two for himself, two for his wife, and two for each of the children – making eight in all. Never more, never less. Biography for him, usually, thrillers for her, always, and, well, whatever he thinks the children will like. Nearly always round about six thirty. Doesn't take him long: five minutes, ten minutes. Very decisive. 'Evening. Thank you.' Then, 'Thank you. Night.' Doesn't waste words. Nice face, though. Doesn't shave very well, actually. Perhaps he's one of those who shave at night. Shouldn't think so, though. Out of character. Or perhaps he's a twice-a-day man and hasn't got round to it by six thirty. Nice eyes too. Nice everything, in fact. Once he *did* open up a bit. Left a letter in one of his books. Gave it back to him the next week. It was very interesting, actually: from his sister. Anyway, 'You left this in your book,' I said. 'Oh,' he said. 'Thank you. Thank you very much. I wondered what had happened to it.' But that was quite a long time ago. Probably six or seven months. Anyway, as I say, I don't mind changing with you any *other* night, Susie, but not Tuesday. The Tuesday *after* would be all right, of course, if you like.

Monologue 12: Questions

Listen to the monologue and then answer the questions.

1. Who is the speaker?
2. Who is the listener?
3. Who is 'he'?
4. At what time does he usually come?
5. How long does he stay?
6. What does he always take for his wife?
7. Does he always take biography for himself?
8. How many children has he?
9. Apart from 'nice', what other adjective does the speaker use to describe him?
10. What doesn't he waste?
11. What doesn't he do very well?
12. 'It was very interesting, actually.'
    a) What was interesting?
    b) What does this remark imply that the speaker has done?
13. What has the listener asked the speaker to agree to do?
14. Why is the speaker not prepared to do this?
15. Why will the Tuesday *after* be all right?

Monologue 13

Well, Mr March, I suppose the first thing I ought to do is to offer my congratulations. I saw the photograph in the local paper, you know. Looking younger every day, if I may say so. And if I may say, furthermore, you're a very lucky man – such an *attractive* young lady. By the way, I hope you won't misunderstand what happened just now. Miss Hobbs – that's the girl you saw out there – she's new, you know. And though she's a very *nice* girl, she still has a few things to learn about how to, er . . . But she *was* acting on my instructions, let me hasten to add, because I was hoping you might spare me a moment. And though there's nothing to worry about at this stage, we *have* been just a little bit concerned, actually, especially as you've been with us for over fifty years, and throughout that time you've always had a healthy balance in your favour. And then, suddenly, there was this – yes, here it is – which, of course, we covered without question. And now there's this – which is rather large. So, I'm just wondering . . . I can let it go through, of course. But I thought that, bearing in mind that you've now – how shall I put it? – opened a new chapter in your life, you might welcome an opportunity for a word.

Monologue 13: Questions

Listen to the monologue and then answer the questions.

1. Who is the speaker?
2. In what place is the speaker talking?
3. Who, in a word, is Mr March?
4. Who is Miss Hobbs?
5. What does she still need to learn?
6. Suggest what she probably said.
7. What 'new chapter' has Mr March recently 'opened'?
8. What photograph did the speaker see?
9. What has Mr March had in his favour for over fifty years?
10. What are the two items which the speaker draws to Mr March's attention?
11. What action has the speaker taken in the case of
    a) the first item?
    b) the second item?
12. In a sentence or two, say what the speaker's general aim is in this monologue.

Monologue 14

Oh, it was very nice, Joanna. Not the sort of thing you'd have enjoyed, of course. We just sat and talked most of the time. The food didn't come for ages, though. In fact I began to wish I'd had something before I went. But it was very nice when it came. Well, in a *way* it was. Though she *will* insist on trying out those fancy recipes! And the coffee! You know, I don't know why it is I always get stuck with Mike Green. He's all right, of course. And I believe he's marvellous at his job. But he will insist on talking about it *all* the time, and, well, sewage engineering has *limited* appeal for me. Well, it was a buffet supper, as you know, so as I'd been sitting next to him *all* the time until the food came, I'd hoped to get away, but he stuck like glue! Oh, well. It wasn't bad, really. How about you? Did you shorten your dress? Gosh, I'm tired. See you in the morning. Oh, dear! Sorry! Do please excuse me. I thought the bathroom was free! Joanna, who's that? I thought you said you were having a *quiet* evening!

Monologue 14: Questions

Listen to the monologue and then answer the questions.

1. Why does the speaker think Joanna would not have enjoyed the evening she describes?
2. What complaints does the speaker have about the food?
3. 'And the coffee!' Explain this remark.
4. What has '*limited* appeal' for the speaker?
5. What is the speaker's complaint about Mike Green?
6. How long did Mike Green 'stick like glue'?
7. 'Oh, it was very nice.'
   This is the speaker's first remark about the evening. In her last remark about it, she modifies this opinion to what?
8. What was the listener intending to do that evening?
9. Where has the speaker gone when she says 'Oh, dear! Sorry!'?
10. Why does she say this?
11. What conclusion does she come to?

Monologue 15

Well, I know it's midnight and you've come out ten miles. And if you say there isn't any in there – it's completely empty – then that must be the problem – which is a bit embarrassing for me, and a nuisance for you, and I apologise. But even so, what I'm saying is it ought to come under the *guarantee*, you see. Look – before you put any in – I'll switch on and show you. Now. You see. It isn't even *in* the red section! And according to the book – I can show you, if you like – that means there's at least a gallon! At least! Well, dammit, it's only two weeks old, and, as I say, it says 'mechanical defects'. Well, what I'm saying is it *is* a mechanical defect. I mean, if it indicates one thing and means another, that's not my fault, is it? I mean, the red should mean what it says, shouldn't it? Anyway, now you've seen it with your own eyes, so you can put some in, will you? Lucky you brought it, actually, isn't it? By the way, I'll pay you for *that*, of course – that's obviously not covered. Oh, hell – now it's starting to rain. Marvellous, isn't it! Here, where are you going? Hey, come back! O.K., O.K. All right – how much do you want, then?

Monologue 15: Questions

Listen to the monologue and then answer the questions.

1. Who is the listener?
2. Who is the speaker?
3. What is the problem, according to the listener?
4. Why is this embarrassing for the speaker?
5. What, according to the speaker
   a) should be covered by the guarantee?
   b) shouldn't be covered by the guarantee?
6. How has the problem arisen, according to the speaker?
7. Why does the speaker 'switch on and show' the listener *before* she lets the listener 'put any in'?
8. What does the speaker mean by *it* in each of the following:
   a) it's completely empty
   b) It isn't even *in* the red section!
   c) it's only two weeks old
   d) it says 'mechanical defects'
   e) Lucky you brought it.
9. Why was it 'lucky' that he brought it?
10. 'Hey, come back!'
    Explain.
11. 'All right—how much do you want, then?'
    Explain.
12. Suggest what the outcome will be.

Monologue 16

We've got some marvellous tapes and marvellous food, and lots to drink. I *know* it started two hours ago, but there's plenty left, and it's bound to go on till two or three. No problem about transport – either way. We asked Dave and Susan up – though I'm not too keen on *her* – so *they* won't complain. And the couple upstairs are off for the weekend. So, as I say, there's no problem. Perhaps it'll go on till . . . Anyway, we can give you breakfast. What? I don't believe you. And even if you *are*, it's only eleven, so jolly well get up again. And it's no use telling me *that*, because I know that isn't the reason at all – *I* know what the reason is, and it's nothing to do with what you say. Well, you've no need to worry – Sam *did* come. And I should've known better – but the fact is, I'd forgotten that you and he . . . and anyway I don't think it'll last, Jane. In fact, I'm willing to bet that in a week or two, you'll both be . . . But as I say, he's gone now, or I wouldn't have rung. So you *can* come. What d'you say? Well, I can get him *back*, if you like.

Monologue 16: Questions

Listen to the monologue and then answer the questions.

1. What event is taking place?
2. When did it start?
3. Who is the speaker?
4. Where is the speaker?
5. Where is the listener?
6. 'there's plenty left'
   Plenty of what?
7. Who are Dave and Susan?
8. What *might* Dave and Susan have done, in other circumstances?
9. Why are they unlikely to do so?
10. What is the speaker's main aim in this monologue?
11. Suggest what the listener says which causes the speaker to say
    'I don't believe you.'
12. '*I* know what the reason is.'
    The reason for what?
13. '*I* know what the reason is.'
    What *is* the reason, according to the speaker?
14. 'Sam *did* come.'
    What is implied by the extra stress on *did*?
15. 'I'm willing to bet that in a week or two, you'll both be . . .'
    a) Who are 'both'?
    b) Suggest a completion for the sentence.
16. 'What d'you say?'
    What point is the listener making when the speaker asks this
    question?

Monologue 17

It's a very old crystal ball, actually. Been in our family for five
generations, but it's got a crack in it, unfortunately. Got it in my
grandmother's time. You see? Here. See it? It was a certain Colonel
Wilkins. Didn't like what she said, you see. Overturned the table
and went out in a *terrible* temper. Came back the following week and
apologised. Charming man, apparently. Well it seems she'd *told* him
not to go to the city, you see. Had the scar for the rest of his life,
poor man. Nothing very serious, fortunately. The station clock, it
was. Big clock. Quite famous – you know the one I mean. Well,
one of the hands dropped off, you see. The hour hand, actually. Of
course, he offered to buy her a new one, but she told him not to
bother. So here it is. Well, now, as this is our first session, I suppose I
ought to ask you a few questions. Well, no. No, I ought to do the
job properly, didn't I? Now. Yes, let me see. Mm. Yes, your name is
Peter Brown, 46 years old, assistant bank manager, married, one boy,
one girl – no, two – and a parrot, and you like gardening and you
play cards every Tuesday and Friday with some friends called
Newton, no Newberry. Right? And on a Sunday . . . Yes, every
Sunday, you . . . Oh. Mm. Ah. Well, well, well, well, well. Mm!
Yes, you're a bellringer, aren't you? You ring one of the bells at the
church, don't you? Mm? Yes. Well, this is the point: next Sunday,
stay in bed. Right?

Monologue 17: Questions

Listen to the monologue and then answer the questions.

1. What is the speaker's occupation?
2. Where does this scene take place?
3. What is the listener's name and occupation?
4. 'Got it in my grandmother's time.'
   What is 'it'?
5. 'Didn't like what she said.'
   a) Who didn't like this?
   b) Who said it?
   c) What was said?
6. How did he get the scar?
7. What is the possible significance of specifying the *hour* hand?
8. 'he offered to buy her a new one'
   A new what?
9. How many girls has the listener?
10. Who does he play cards with?
11. What pet has he got?
12. What does he do on a Sunday?
13. 'Well, this is the point.'
    Explain the point.

Monologue 18

You're absolutely right – we *have* met. And I do remember you very well. You usually sit next to the Chairman, I seem to recall. In fact I think you've sat there on each occasion I've applied. Yes – the first was for one in Africa, which I didn't get. The second was for one in Asia. Didn't get that either. The third was for one in South America. But I keep on trying, you know – and in the meantime, I don't starve, of course. And, well, I still like it here anyway. There's no place like home, after all, is there? But it would be nice, even so, if *this* time . . . You know, I didn't know you lived in our part of the world. I think you'll agree this really is the best train, isn't it? Far better than the eight thirty. Three hundred miles. No stops. Gets you there in no time. Oh, good. Shall we have some? The buffet gets rather crowded – best to have it here, probably. Yes – two, please. White? Oh, sorry – it's *all* white, anyway. Sugar? Yes, as I say, I don't quite seem to be what they're looking for, but I do keep on trying. It must be *very* interesting to be on the other side of the fence, as it were. I mean, I wouldn't know what to ask: 'Mr er . . ., can you tell us *exactly* why you want to go to, er . . . er . . . And tell us *exactly* why you think you are the person we should, er . . . Ahem. Ahem.' Worse still, I never seem to know what to answer! Anyway, *this* one is in Australia. They're looking for . . . But I expect you know. That *is* where you're going, I suppose?

Monologue 18: Questions

Listen to the monologue and then answer the questions.

1. In what place is the speaker talking?
2. Where have the speaker and the listener met previously?
3. What were their respective roles then?
4. Where is the speaker going?
5. How much do we know about where the *listener* is going?
6. 'Shall we have some?'
   What does 'some' refer to?
7. 'it's *all* white, anyway'
   Explain this remark.
8. What does the speaker mean by 'the other side of the fence'?
9. What is the speaker doing when he uses a different voice?
10. 'But I expect you know.'
    What does he expect the listener will know?
11. 'That *is* where you're going, I suppose?'
    What place does the speaker have in mind?
12. In what connection does the speaker mention Africa, Asia and South America?

Monologue 19

Yes, I agree. Lovely breakfast. Very nice. Excellent coffee, especially, don't you think? Anyway, as I was telling you, it happens to me every time I go to a new place: I always end up paying twice or three times as much as I should for the first ride. But last night was the worst ever. The train got in at about eleven, so I felt lucky to get one – though it looked a bit old and battered. But *he* was *so* polite – and you don't get much of that *these* days: 'Let me take your bags,' he says. 'No trouble,' he says. 'It's a hot, sticky night,' he says, 'but don't worry, madam, it's air-conditioned,' – and it *was*, surprisingly – 'just relax and I'll get you there in no time.' So we went for miles down this road and that road and he pointed out all sorts of buildings and other sights that he said I'd appreciate when I could see them properly in the morning. And he told me that though this was one of the few cities in the world where a woman could go at that time of night on her own and nothing to fear, even so, it was a good thing I'd taken a *registered* vehicle, because you never knew, did you? Though *I* couldn't see any special registration number or anything, and I didn't think to make a note of his licence plate – and it wouldn't have made any difference, I don't suppose. So here I am. And as you can see, if you look out of the window, that's the station! Just across the road! Anyway. Well, it's a lovely hotel, isn't it? Are you on holiday too?

Monologue 19: Questions

Listen to the monologue and then answer the questions.

1. In what place is the speaker talking?
2. What has she just had?
3. Who is the listener?
4. Are the speaker and the listener well known to each other?
5. When did the events the speaker describes occur?
6. When does 'it' always happen to the speaker?
7. What does she end up paying?
8. 'I felt lucky to get one.'
   To get what?
9. Who is 'he'?
10. Why was the speaker surprised that it was air-conditioned?
11. 'I'll get you there in no time.'
    Where is *there* specifically?
12. Why was the speaker not expected to appreciate the buildings fully on the occasion described?
13. 'all sorts of buildings and other . . .'
    Is the missing word spelled 'site', or 'sight'?
    Give reasons.
14. Why did he say the speaker was *particularly* safe?
15. What might have happened if she had noted the details on his number plate?
16. 'that's the station! Just across the road!' What is the significance of these words?
17. What do you think the speaker will probably *do* about the incident?

Monologue 20

Now, let me just go over this again, just to be sure I've got it right. The wall is the one between your property and his. But it's actually entirely on your land, and it belongs to you. And what he's done is to remove that part of his garden that runs alongside – that's to say he's removed the soil to such a level that there's inadequate support on his side. And he's put concrete in its place, but you claim the amount of concrete he's laid doesn't suffice. In fact it's started to lean already, because it's being pushed from your side, where the soil is at the original level. I suppose you're right about the wind: it gets very wild up there in winter, doesn't it? It *could* happen, certainly, as you say. And if it were to damage his *car*, that would introduce complications, too, wouldn't it? Well, all right, Mrs Macdonald – I've got it, I think. And you're perfectly correct: though it's your wall, he has *no* right to remove the support on his side. Well, leave it with me. I'll send him a letter. But, you know, in these cases it's often better to have a word yourself, first. Oh, you have. And what did he say? Mm. You've had rather a lot of trouble, haven't you? Not only about *this*, I mean. Well, as I say, I'll get it off today. What? Well . . . Oh, yes. Yes, you *could* of course – but that's a bit *extreme*, isn't it? I mean, I know he's awkward, but . . . Well, I wouldn't rush into it if I were you. The market isn't very good just now. And if you do, before he's put it right, I'd have to point it out to any intending purchaser, you see. Well, it's nothing much, true – but it *might* put them off, you know.

Monologue 20: Questions

Listen to the monologue and then answer the questions.

1. Who is the speaker?
2. Who is the listener?
3. Who is 'he'?
4. Where is the wall?
5. Who owns it?
6. What has 'he' removed?
7. What has he put in its place?
8. What does the listener think of this replacement?
9. 'It *could* happen, certainly.'
   What could happen, and why?
10. 'that would introduce complications'
    a) What is 'that'?
    b) What would the complications be?
11. 'Well, as I say, I'll get it off today.'
    Get what off today?
12. What course of action is 'often better', according to the speaker?
13. 'Oh, you have. And what did he say?'
    What sort of thing did he probably say?
14. What course of action is the listener contemplating, which the speaker thinks 'a bit extreme'?
15. 'The market isn't very good just now.'
    For what?
16. What would the speaker have to point out?

40

Monologue 21

Well, sir, I know you'll think I'm crazy. After all, five years is a long time. And now that it's come, you'd think I wouldn't be able to wait. And until last night that was exactly the way I felt. But then I started thinking. Well, it isn't an ideal life – nobody'd say it is. It's very hard, and there's a lot about it that quite honestly I've found very hard to bear. But on the other hand I've got into the routine, you know: exercise in the morning; regular work in the laundry; a small allowance for cigarettes; plenty of sleep; Frank, or Jim or Ted peeping through the grille, just to check. And the lads: good company, you know. And I know Michael deserved everything he got – though he says he was innocent – but he's been very good to me. Excellent conversationalist. Likes to be tidy, too, just as I do. We've never had an argument, let alone a fight. Look, I know there's a limit to what you can do, sir. But I was thinking: Well, the day before Christmas is just a bit too much. Can't you manage just another couple of days? Nobody'll notice. Then I'll be off, of course. Two days? One day . . .?

Monologue 21 : Questions

Listen to the monologue and then answer the questions.

1. Who is the speaker?
2. Who is the listener?
3. In what place is the speaker talking?
4. What is due to happen on the day before Christmas?
5. What is the speaker asking for?
6. Why should this be thought 'crazy'?
7. 'I've got into the routine.'
   What *work* is a part of this routine?
8. a) Who are Frank, Jim and Ted?
   b) What do they do, 'just to check'?
9. Who are 'the lads'?
10. Who is Michael?
11. What two things does the speaker particularly like about Michael?
12. What is the one thing on which he has an opinion differing from Michael's?
13. 'Until last night that was exactly the way I felt.'
    What had the speaker 'felt'?
14. What *movement* do you think the listener probably made when the speaker said, 'Two days?'

No, no, it's not fair to say I disapprove. Disappointed, perhaps. But, anyway, nothing I say is likely to make any difference, is it? I mean, you've made your mind up already, haven't you? It's just that, well, I'd always thought it would turn out differently. We've always had a particular way of life, done certain things, moved in certain circles. No, I don't disapprove. I don't really know him, anyway, do I? So how can I disapprove? But what about Billy? You've told him, I suppose? You know, I'd always somehow expected it would be Billy. It seemed so natural. So suitable. I suppose the merger will be out of the question, now. I know it's in your *father's* interest to go through with it. And I'm certain it's in theirs. But you and Billy: that would have acted as . . . well, it would have been the *cement*, if I could put it that way. You *have* told him, have you? And you say you'll have to support *him* for a while. Well, these days I suppose that's all right, though in *my* time . . . Of course, in the old days I would have told you – or your father would – that you couldn't expect a penny from us, and that would have been that. In most cases *that* helped us to see sense. I certainly did. Oh, yes – it may surprise you to know there *was* someone. But my father made the position quite clear, and I felt I had no alternative – not *really* an alternative. Anyway, we've been reasonably happy, your father and me. I'm sure we have. But, as you say, we must be realistic these days. We can't use *that* weapon. And we're so proud of your success. Well, as I say, we don't know him very well. And of course the answer to your question is 'yes'. Why not tonight, for dinner?

Monologue 22: Questions

Listen to the monologue and then answer the questions.

1. Who are the speaker and the listener?
2. What is the listener proposing to do?
3. Why had the speaker 'expected it would be Billy'?
4. What word does the speaker prefer to 'disapprove'?
5. What 'merger' has been proposed?
6. Is the merger now out of the question?
7. What does the speaker have to admit is probably 'all right' these days, though it would not have been in her time?
8. What course of action was usually effective in such circumstances in the old days?
9. Why would such a course not be practicable in the present situation?
10. What do you think the listener's *question* to the speaker was?
11. 'It may surprise you to know there *was* someone.'
    Explain this remark.
12. What kind of married relationship has the speaker had?

Yes, but all I mean to say is that there's nothing *special* about yours, John. Very undistinguished, yours are. Very ordinary. Relatively speaking, that is. But you'll see next Thursday when he brings the students in, it'll be *mine* they'll spend all the time over. 'Now, Mr Bartholomew,' he'll say. 'What do you make of those? What've you got to say about the colour? Notice the texture. And above all, note the distribution.' 'Cos it's the *distribution* more than anything, you see. *That's* what seems to intrigue them. You see, yours are here, here and here, just the same as everybody else's are: Joe's are, and Bill's are – and everybody else's. But you see, *mine* are not here, here and here – they're here, here and *here*. And that's what's unique. That's what makes me the star attraction. Oh, but I'll tell you this: they're itching *terribly* today. Now yours *don't* itch much, do they? I think I shall ask her to put something on. Well, no. I'll wait half an hour, because they change over at half past one, and then *she'll* be on. *Very* nice, isn't she? Lovely. Could've been a model, I reckon. And then it'll be two o'clock – but she isn't coming today. Can't say it bothers me too much. Talks about her back most of the time. Well, I know it doesn't get any better. But in the circumstances that isn't really the idea, is it? Always brings some nice fruit, though. What about yours? Is she coming, John? Actually, at first I thought you were single, you know. Hey, look at *him*! Look at that *new* fellow! See – he's got his jacket off, and I do believe . . . Oh, no. No, it's all right. Nothing to worry about. I thought for a moment . . . No – quite normal.

Monologue 23: Questions

Listen to the monologue and then answer the questions.

1. Who is the speaker?
2. In what place is he talking?
3. Who is the listener?
4. In a word, what is the speaker's main topic?
5. In one word, what does the speaker claim to be, in comparison with the others?
6. What characteristic *particularly* distinguishes him from the others?
7. Who is Mr Bartholomew?
8. Who is supposed to be addressing Mr Bartholomew?
9. 'I think I shall ask her to put something on.'
   a) Who is 'she'?
   b) Explain 'put something on'.
10. Why does he decide not to ask her?
11. What is the significance of two o'clock?
12. 'she isn't coming today'
    Who is 'she'?
13. 'that isn't really the idea, is it?'
    Explain this remark.
14. 'What about yours?'
    Who does 'yours' refer to?
15. 'Nothing to worry about. I thought for a moment . . .'
    What did the speaker think?

Monologue 24

Well, Mr Peterson, we've now been able to give full consideration to your offer. And I want you to know that we're extremely impressed with your lucid, challenging and interesting analysis of our needs as you see them. And I may say it's an interpretation with which many of us here have a great deal of sympathy. Furthermore we're *entirely* convinced that you have the resources of men, materials and expertise to respond to those needs, and – and this is an important consideration for *us* – respond to them within the *extremely* tight deadlines to which we must work. Again, we can say, without reservation, that in all our dealings with a great many organisations we have never been provided with a set of estimates which seem to us so comprehensive, competitive and realistic. Lastly, I wish to say we've been delighted at the quality of the personal relationships you and your team have generated here during your short time with us. Well, now, having said all this – and I know that everyone in this room will want to be associated with my words – it is particularly difficult for me to have to tell you . . .

Monologue 24: Questions

Listen to the monologue and then answer the questions.

1. In what place is the speaker talking?
2. Who is the speaker?
3. To whom are his remarks addressed?
4. Who else is present?
5. What has the speaker given full consideration to?
6. With what three adjectives does he describe the 'analysis'?
7. What has been the reaction to 'the interpretation'?
8. What necessary resources does the listener have, according to the speaker?
9. What capability in deploying these resources does he have, according to the speaker?
10. What does the speaker describe as 'comprehensive, competitive and realistic'?
11. In what other field have the team proved successful?
12. Suggest a completion for the speaker's last sentence.
13. What is the speaker's overall aim in this monologue?

Answers

Monologue 1 : Answers

1. A lift (elevator).
2. A secretary.
3. The lift has broken down.
4. Not very well – though he knows who she works for.
5. The light has gone out.
6. She has stepped on his feet.
7. The lift.
8. When he arrives in the morning and goes up in the lift he has his lunchtime sandwiches with him.
   Note The word 'have' here presumably does not mean *eat*.
9. It's not very exciting, and it's very expensive.
10. The listener.
11. a) The speaker's wife, presumably.
    b) Ballet.
12. a) The lift.
    b) It is not a totally enclosed box.
13. The speaker's secretary.
14. They have already shouted for help.

Monologue 2: Answers

1. A surgery, or consulting room.
2. A doctor.
3. 'Practice', 'prescribe' and 'sickness'. Additionally, the word 'colleague' helps to establish that the listener is not the speaker's regular doctor.
4. Sleeping pills (or a prescription for these).
5. The doctor is not willing to prescribe any.
6. One.
7. Though an insomniac, she fell asleep during her favourite programme. This was funny because one would not expect anyone – especially an insomniac – to do this.

   Note a) The word 'funny' refers to the situation and not to the television programme.

   b) 'Funny' probably means 'strange' or 'peculiar' more than it means 'humorous'.
8. Pins and needles.
9. The speaker's regular doctor.
10. The waiting room.
11. The remaining patients.
12. The speaker's initial reaction is one of surprise and slight indignation. She then concedes that perhaps she could and should discontinue the treatment. This admission, however, is complicated by thoughts of what her regular doctor's response will be.

Monologue 3: Answers

1. An organisation.
2. He is his superior (e.g. the chairman or manager).
3. Charles.
4. To dismiss Charles and retain Tim.
5. Charles and Tim.
6. Two employees, seemingly in positions of responsibility, have proved unable to work together amicably.
7. '. . . had reached the stage . . .'
8. Compensation.
9. Unique.
10. The document containing the severance terms.
11. The pronoun 'it' refers here to the whole situation, not merely to compensation.
12. '. . . that's it . . .'
13. There are many possible completions along the lines of:
    couldn't/didn't get on (together)
    didn't hit it off
    couldn't work together
14. To terminate the listener's appointment in as tactful and painless a way as possible.

Monologue 4: Answers

1. An art gallery, or exhibition room.
2. Painting (possibly and/or drawing. Less likely, photography).
3. The proprietor of the gallery, or the agent, who has arranged the exhibition.
4. a) The paintings.
   b) In the attic.
5. The exhibition.
6. That the pictures to which they are attached have been sold.
7. a) A visitor to the exhibition.
   b) The artist (i.e. the speaker).
8. Don't admit it.
9. She has been known to the artist for at least ten years, since she is the subject of one of his portraits. She seems to be famous, and according to the speaker has retained her looks. The phrase 'as I keep on telling you' suggests a continuing and possibly fond relationship.
10. Because of the clever lighting, the glossy catalogue, and the smart people.

Monologue 5: Answers

1. Her husband, presumably.
2. The hairdresser.
3. Cut off too much of her hair.
4. Relaxing. Daydreaming.
5. She has had her hair satisfactorily cut there on previous occasions.
6. She will never patronise that hairdresser again.
7. He smiles.
8. To visit her in-laws.
9. Her sister-in-law's.
10. They prefer their son not to be accompanied by his wife. She doesn't like her mother-in-law's cooking.
11. A cold.

Monologue 6: Answers

1. (Male) students.
2. Alan.
3. Examinations.
4. He works steadily and methodically throughout the term.
5. A period of guilt and anxiety followed by 'the panic stage'.
6. Hardly any.
7. He takes aspirins occasionally.
8. Four.
9. The speaker's girl friend.
10. Perhaps he would go off for the weekend.
11. A restaurant or snack-bar, or perhaps a pub.
12. Passed.
13. Presumably a textbook or article.
14. a) The speaker's way of approaching examinations.
    b) 'One' or 'anyone'. The main point is that 'you' does *not* refer directly to the *listener*.

Monologue 7: Answers

1. The manager, or chief executive.
2. 'Quiet', 'shy' and 'pretty'.
3. That she will be the boss.
4. 'Bossy' and 'aggressive'.
5. The deputy manager.
6. The accountant.
7. Her merits.
8. A job.
9. He's the best man in the business, he's just what they need, and the deputy manager has already approved.
10. If each had known who – or what – the other was.
11. Not to appoint the listener.
12. She seems to think that the personal relationship they have developed would make a proper working relationship impossible.
13. She has no regrets.

Monologue 8: Answers

1. The vicar, or parson, or priest.
2. The church hall.
3. The audience.
4. A concert or show.
5. The audience.
6. They have got wet.
7. With understanding and cheerful good humour.
8. The roof of the church.
9. The roof of the church hall.
10. The surveyor.
11. An appeal for donations, presumably.
12. After the service tomorrow.
13. Wet.
14. Receptacles, or containers.
15. The floor may get damaged, and this would involve even greater expense.

Monologue 9: Answers

1. Frank.
2. Himself.
3. Ordinary.
4. In a plane.
5. Hijack the plane.
6. To become involved in a conversation.
7. Security men, or possibly customs officers.
8. An air hostess.
9. A female passenger.
10. She is good looking – even if she drinks a lot.
11. They didn't look in the place where his weapon is concealed.
12. The man in the next seat.
13. He is impressed with the smallness of the weapon.
14. Security guards.
15. What he is going to say to the passengers and crew when he hijacks the plane.

Monologue 10 : Answers

1. Get jobs (as secretaries).
2. No.
3. Typing (shorthand?), filing, and handling the telephone.
4. Her appearance.
5. Neat, alert, obedient, and dependable in a crisis.
6. The prospective employer.
7. Travel.
8. For lunch.
9. Probably his wife.
10. The restaurant, or pub, where they had lunch.
11. Dinner and travel.
12. The listener's neat blouse.
13. Probably not, since they are making chips.
14. She probably shrugs or shakes her head, to indicate her lack of success.

Monologue 11 : Answers

1. A lecture room.
2. The lecturer.
3. Undergraduate students.
4. To introduce the course.
5. To check the attendance.
6. The attendance is much larger than anticipated.
7. That the subject *does* attract interest at *post-graduate* levels.
8. A catalyst.
9. A neat exposition plus handouts, etc.
10. The derivation of the name of the subject.
11. It seems there has been a notice announcing a change in the location of lectures. Presumably most of the students present have missed this notice and have therefore attended the wrong lecture.

Monologue 12: Answers

1. A librarian.
2. Another librarian.
3. A borrower.
4. About six thirty.
5. Five or ten minutes.
6. Thrillers.
7. No – though he usually does.
8. Two (he takes two books for each).
9. Decisive.
10. Words.
11. Shave.
12. a) Either the situation generally, or the letter specifically.
    b) Read the letter.
13. Exchange duties.
14. She wishes to be on duty when the man comes to the library.
15. Because he only comes on alternate Tuesdays.

Monologue 13: Answers

1. A bank manager.
2. His office.
3. A customer.
4. A new employee – a junior employee, probably.
5. Tact, it appears.
6. Something along the lines of:
   The manager wants to see you.
   We've been told not to cash any more of your cheques.
   You're in for trouble.
7. He has married.
8. The wedding photograph.
9. A healthy balance.
10. Either two actual cheques or two entries. Or perhaps one entry and one uncleared cheque.
11. a) Cleared it without question.
    b) Held it up, pending an interview with the drawer of the cheque.
12. Presumably he aims to discover tactfully how Mr March intends to conduct his affairs now that he is married. Also to point out, diplomatically but no doubt firmly, what the limits are.

Monologue 14: Answers

1. Presumably it would have been too dull.
2. The hostess had been trying out 'fancy' recipes. Also the food was late.
3. The coffee was terrible.
4. Sewage engineering.
5. He talks about his work all the time.
6. Throughout the evening.
7. 'It wasn't bad, really.'
8. Shorten her dress.
9. To the bathroom.
10. Someone is in there.
11. That Joanna has not had a quiet evening.

Monologue 15: Answers

1. A mechanic.
2. The driver of the vehicle.
   Note a) One probably assumes the vehicle is a car, though it could be something else, e.g. a motor bike.
   b) The monologue does not definitely establish that the speaker *owns* the vehicle.
3. The car has simply run out of petrol.
4. The speaker has called the mechanic out to attend to a break-down. Now that she has been told the car is out of petrol, she feels foolish and probably even guilty.
5. a) The mechanic's charges for coming out to the vehicle and identifying the problem. (Later, presumably, he will also claim the cost of re-calibrating, repairing, or replacing the fuel gauge.)
   b) The actual cost of the petrol.
6. The fuel gauge has given a false reading indicating that at least a gallon of petrol remains in the tank – which is in fact empty.
7. She wishes to prove to the mechanic that the gauge indicates that there is petrol, even though the tank is empty. (Once the petrol is put into the tank, the fault will be more difficult to demonstrate.)
8. a) The fuel tank.
   b) The needle of the petrol gauge.
   c) The vehicle.
   d) The guarantee.
   e) The petrol.
9. The mechanic would certainly have brought tools and probably certain spare parts, but not necessarily petrol.
10. The listener does not seem to accept that his charges should be collected under the guarantee, and starts to leave without having put in the petrol. This is probably his means of forcing the issue. He knows he is in a strong position.
11. The speaker recognises that she is at the mechanic's mercy, so she asks him what his total charges are.
12. Presumably the speaker will pay all the charges in order to get home. Later she will probably make a claim under the guarantee.

Monologue 16: Answers

1. A party.
2. Two hours ago.
3. The host.
4. At the telephone, in her flat.
5. At home.
6. Food and drink.
7. Their neighbours – the occupants of the downstairs flat.
8. Complained about the noise.
9. They have been invited.
10. To persuade the listener to come to the party.
11. Something along the lines of:
    I'm in bed.
    I was asleep when you rang.
    I'd gone to bed.
12. Her absence from the party.
13. She didn't want to encounter Sam.
14. Though he was at the party, he has now left.
15. a) Sam and the listener (Jane).
    b) Something along the lines of:
       together again
       back where you were
       as close as ever
16. That she wished Sam to be there after all.

Monologue 17: Answers

1. Fortune-teller. Crystal-gazer.
2. Wherever the consultation is: probably the fortune-teller's room, but it could be at the listener's house if she visits clients.
3. Peter Brown. Assistant bank manager.
4. The crystal ball.
5. a) Colonel Wilkins.
   b) The fortune-teller's grandmother.
   c) He should not go to the city.
6. The hand of the station clock fell on him.
7. Presumably it was shorter than the minute hand and may therefore have been lighter.
8. Crystal ball.
9. Two.
10. Some friends called Newberry.
11. A parrot.
12. He rings one of the bells at the church – he is a bellringer.
13. If he goes to church the following Sunday, the bell will fall on him (or perhaps only the clapper of the bell).

Monologue 18: Answers

1. A train. Railway compartment.
2. At a number of interviews.
3. The speaker was the applicant, and the listener a member of the selection board.
4. To an interview.
5. He is definitely going to the train's destination. The likelihood is that as this is the day the interviewing board meets and he seems to be a regular member of it, he too is going there.
6. Coffee.
7. No black coffee is available.
8. In the position of interviewer.
9. He is pretending to be the interviewer.
10. The details of the job in Australia.
11. The place where the interview is to be held.
12. In connection with posts for which he has applied unsuccessfully.

Monologue 19: Answers

1. A hotel, restaurant, dining room, or coffee shop.
2. Breakfast.
3. Another guest at the hotel.
4. The fact that the speaker doesn't know whether the listener is on holiday suggests they do not know each other well. But we can't be certain.
5. The previous night.
6. On first arrival in a new place.
7. Twice or three times too much.
8. A taxi.
9. The driver.
10. Because the car was a bit old and battered.
11. Her destination – i.e. her hotel.
12. Because it was dark.
13. 'Sights', presumably. The speaker is on holiday and therefore is probably not interested in property as such. Also the word 'other' suggests 'sight', as a building is not usually termed a 'site'.
14. Because she had hired a 'registered' car.
15. Perhaps the driver could have been traced and she could have got her money back.
16. The driver cheated her by taking her on an unnecessarily long journey, and charged for this.
17. Forget it and get on with her holiday. Put it down to experience.

Monologue 20: Answers

1. A solicitor. A lawyer.
2. A client.
3. The client's neighbour.
4. Between the client's and the neighbour's properties.
5. The client.
6. The soil on his side which was supporting the wall.
7. Some concrete.
8. It is inadequate. It doesn't suffice to support the wall.
9. The wall might collapse as a result of the strong winds.
10. a) If the wall were to fall on the neighbour's car.
    b) The question of responsibility would arise.
11. A letter to the neighbour.
12. It is often better if the parties in the dispute try to settle it themselves by talking about the situation.
13. Something that convinced the client that any further discussion would be pointless.
14. Selling the house.
15. For selling houses.
16. That a dispute existed.

Monologue 21 : Answers

1. A prisoner. A convict.
2. Presumably the Governor.
3. Probably the Governor's office.
4. The speaker is due to be released.
5. To be detained for two more days.
6. The usual expectation is that a prisoner is anxious to be released at the earliest possible moment.
7. Laundry work.
8. a) Warders.
   b) Peep through the grille.
9. Fellow prisoners.
10. The speaker's cell-mate.
11. He is a good conversationalist and he is tidy.
12. The question of Michael's innocence (or guilt).
13. Anxious to be released.
14. He probably shook his head to indicate that the answer was no.

Monologue 22: Answers

1. A mother and daughter.
2. Marry – or live with – someone the mother thinks unsuitable.
3. Billy and the listener shared a common background.
4. Disappointed.
5. Presumably two businesses or organisations with which the listener's family and Billy's family (or associates) are respectively concerned.
6. Not necessarily. The need for the merger remains. Whether it will come about without the marriage to cement it is an open question.
7. For a woman to support a man.
8. The threat to withdraw financial support.
9. The listener appears to be financially independent.
10. Questions along the lines of:
    May I bring him to meet you?
    Can I bring him for a meal?
11. In her time, the speaker thought of marrying a man considered unsuitable for her.
12. A 'reasonably happy' one.